THE END OF DAYS A 30-DAY DEVOTIONAL

WATCHING FOR THE RETURN OF MESSIAH

SHAWN OZBUN

CONTENTS

I SAW A VISION

I heard a loud commotion coming from outside. Walking into my dimly lit living room, I looked through the large windows, peering up to the sky. Observing what looked like a violent, dark storm on the horizon, black and gray clouds filled the sky.

Suddenly, the wall holding the window began to open up, collapsing from the center and disappearing to the left and right. It was as if this world were nothing more than a digital simulation. I then noticed a man wrapped in gold standing before me in the opening of the wall. I called out to him in excitement, "Jesus!" He then took me by the hand. He was no longer wrapped in gold.

I can't remember what he was wearing, but he seemed to take on the appearance of a common man. We took off running to the outside, and it was now sunny and beautiful. However, we seemed to be running over the top of a large lake, or maybe an ocean. There were several people in the water in distress with their hands sticking out as if they needed help. At this point, I was several paces behind Jesus as we run and the gap is getting larger. I desperately wanted to catch up to him so I could ask a question. Although, I was not even sure of the question I had. I felt as though I wanted to ask him if this moment was the end, if this was the rapture, had he finally come for us?

As I am running, trying with all my might to catch up to Jesus, I run past a man with his hand up out of the water. The man is near me so I reach down and pull him up out of the water as I run past. He then begins running behind me in my pursuit to catch Jesus. Finally, Jesus comes to a stop and I catch up to him. However, before I can ask Jesus my important question, he tells me, "I just want you to be happy with the life I've given you." And just like that, I awoke from the night vision.

The year was 2012, and this was no ordinary dream. You would be hard pressed trying to convince me it was not a vision from God. Admittedly, it was a strange message and it would be years later before I would come to realize its meaning.

I've never had a dream this vivid, this real, which remained in my mind forever. I thought it strange at first and for several years after. Why would Jesus take the time to give me a vision? Simply for the sake of saying He wants me to be happy with the life He has given me? No, it couldn't be.

A couple years later, I created my podcast entitled Truthfed, or as it's now known, Scripture and Prophecy. I would begin chasing after Jesus, and I would invite others to come out of the world and join me in this pursuit. A pursuit after our King and a desire to watch for His coming.

I should note, I am far from perfect, nor I am worthy of this calling. Why God would give a person such as myself a wonderful vision and give me a work for His kingdom is beyond my understanding.

I pray this book will enlighten you and give you a great desire to remain awake and watching for the King of Kings and the Lord of Lords. I believe there has never been a time such as the one we are living in, and I believe His return is very, very near.

We are living in the most interesting time in history. At least, the most interesting since the times of Noah. I believe it to be the last days. Many have believed this to be true. There are countless books and DVDs being sold to the American Church about the times we are living in. Everyone seems to have their own charts, graphs and diagrams predicting the order of events. We are being told tribulation is coming, but don't worry, you will be raptured first. Others say there is no rapture, expect to see the Antichrist first and the world burning down around you.

I can't help but wonder, are any of these timelines correct? Do we have it all figured out? Do we need to wait for a third temple and an Antichrist before we should even hope to see our Savior's return?

I fear many have taken their eyes off of Jesus. They have taken their attention away from the scriptures and what Jesus himself said about His return. They have replaced the facts of the scriptures and the promises of Christ with false and trendy End Times doctrines of men. Therefore, they have been lead astray. The blind leading the blind.

I believe the scriptures tell us we are to be ready and watching at all times. There is a great reward for those who persist in watching zealously for His appearing and great judgement for those who are caught off guard. Great promises for those He finds watching and working. Great punishment for those who allow themselves to be lured back into the temptations of this world, thinking His return is delayed or in the distant future.

In this book, we are going to examine from the scriptures what it really means to be watching for the return of our Messiah. It is not my goal to convince you of my End Times theology, only to point your eyes to the Savior.

"COULD YE NOT WATCH WITH ME ONE HOUR?"

DAY 1

One of the most common themes I find in the Gospels, spoken out of the mouth of Jesus to His followers, is to be watching. Be careful you are not caught unaware. We even see this terminology being used with three of the disciples in the Garden of Gethsemane, before Jesus is captured and taken away to be crucified.

In the Matthew account of this event, we find Jesus saying something very interesting to His disciples when He finds them sleeping. This is something I think many of us might miss if we do not pay close attention to His words.

> "And he cometh unto the disciples, and findeth them asleep, and saith unto Peter, **What, could ye not watch with me one hour?** Watch and pray, that ye enter not into temptation: the spirit indeed is willing, but the flesh is weak." Matthew 26:40-41 KJV

I wonder, in a world which seems to be rushing towards the end of days, in a world consumed with distractions, could we be the generation who is caught off guard? Is Jesus asking us today, could ye not watch with me one hour? Are the things of this world really so appealing we are willing to risk missing His coming and being caught unaware?

The digital age has taken our eyes away from what is important and cast our attention on nothingness. Most people can not walk down the street, or even worse, drive a car, without staring into their smart phone. Everywhere we look is a screen begging for our attention. Meanwhile, the ones we love are starved for our attention. Likewise, we are too distracted to pay attention to our Creator and what He might be trying to speak to us.

We are in danger of missing the most important hour of our generation, maybe the most important time in human history. It could be we are living in the last hour right now. We see the signs all around us. However, like the disciples, we are in danger of falling asleep and not understanding the severity of what is about to happen.

I fear we might miss the significance of what Jesus is saying to His disciples. Jesus is warning them about the dangers of not watching, of taking their eyes off Him and the mission at hand. I should also note, it wasn't just the lack of watching which Jesus rebukes His three followers about. He also commands them to be in prayer. He explains there is a real danger which follows if you do not both keep watch and pray.

> "Watch and pray, that ye enter not into temptation: the spirit indeed is willing, but the flesh is weak." Matthew 26:41 KJV

The warning is simple. When you take your eyes off of Him, when you fail to be in prayer, when you let your guard down, you risk falling into temptation. This could be the most important message to this generation. A generation surrounded by temptation and distractions. Never has there been such a great battle for our attention.

LET us never take our eyes off Jesus. His coming is at hand. We must remain in prayer, we must heed His command to watch. Lest we fall to the desires of this world, lest we fall asleep, caught unaware and unprepared for His return. The spirit may be willing, but our flesh is most definitely weak.

THE WISE AND FOOLISH VIRGINS

DAY 2

J esus tells a parable in the book of Matthew, chapter 25. In this parable, Jesus is likening the coming kingdom of heaven to ten virgins, or maidens, who are going forth to meet the bridegroom. Five virgins were wise and were prepared to meet the bridegroom. They took the time to think ahead and be ready. The other five were foolish. They were not prepared and did not think ahead. Unfortunately, for the foolish five, when the shout came at midnight to come out to meet the bridegroom, they could not enter the wedding supper.

"Then shall the kingdom of heaven be likened unto ten virgins, which took their lamps, and went forth to meet the bridegroom. And five of them were wise, and five were foolish. They that were foolish took their lamps, and took no oil with them: But the wise took oil in their vessels with their lamps. While the bridegroom tarried, they all slumbered and slept. And at midnight there was a cry made, Behold, the bridegroom cometh; go ye out to meet him. Then all those virgins arose, and trimmed their lamps. And the foolish said unto the wise, Give us of your oil; for our lamps are gone out. But the wise answered, saying, Not so; lest there be not enough for us and you: but go ye rather to them that sell, and buy for yourselves. And while they went to buy, the bridegroom came; and they that were ready went in with him to the marriage: and the door was shut.

Afterward came also the other virgins, saying, Lord, Lord, open to us. But he answered and said, Verily I say unto you, I know you not. Watch therefore, for ye know neither the day nor the hour wherein the Son of man cometh." Matthew 25:1-13 KJV

The first thing I find interesting is all the virgins fell asleep because the bridegroom failed to come when they were expecting him. He seems delayed. "While the bridegroom tarried, they all slumbered and slept." Matthew 25:5 KJV

This idea of falling asleep seems to come up often when the Bible is talking about being ready and watchful. It seems to warn there is a great danger in taking our eyes off Jesus and falling asleep.

We also see it in the Garden of Gethsemane. Jesus charged His disciples to watch with Him and yet they continued to fall asleep. "And he cometh unto the disciples, and findeth them asleep, and saith unto Peter, What, could ye not watch with me one hour? Watch and pray, that ye enter not into temptation: the spirit indeed is willing, but the flesh is weak." Matthew 26:40-41 KJV

Paul warns us to not sleep as others do, but to watch. "Therefore let us not sleep, as do others; but let us watch and be sober." 1 Thessalonians 5:6 KJV

Jesus wants us to keep our eyes on Him and always be prepared. Lest the world lure us away and we fall back into sin. Lest He come back and finds us unprepared to meet Him and be with Him for all eternity. This is a very serious matter, one which does not get the attention it deserves by the modern church and by modern Christians. Those who dare think in their heart, the Lord has delayed in His coming and slip back into their sinful ways, will not inherit the kingdom. They will instead receive their portion with the hypocrites and the nonbelievers.

> "The lord of that servant shall come in a day when he looketh not for him, and in an hour that he is not aware of, And shall cut him asunder, and appoint him his portion with the hypocrites: there shall be weeping and gnashing of teeth." Matthew 24:50-51 KJV

As you can see, this is a very serious matter and is not to be taken lightly. May we listen to Paul's warning to not sleep, but stay sober and watchful.

OF THAT DAY AND HOUR KNOWETH NO MAN

DAY 3

"The uncertainty of the time of Christ's coming, is, to those who are watchful, a savour of life unto life, and makes them more watchful; but to those who are careless, it is a savour of death unto death, and makes them more careless." - Matthew Henry

WATCHING for the return of Christ is not just some good idea or good Christian practice. It is a commandment from Jesus Himself and commandment which comes with great blessing if obeyed, but with great consequences if ignored.

In the book of Matthew, chapter 24, we see a parable told by Jesus to His followers about the importance of watching and being ready for His return. It tells about the importance of not being caught off guard thinking He has delayed in His coming.

Let's examine the parable verse by verse, starting with verses 42-44.

"Watch therefore: for ye know not what hour your Lord

doth come. But know this, that if the goodman of the house had known in what watch the thief would come, he would have watched, and would not have suffered his house to be broken up. Therefore be ye also ready: for in such an hour as ye think not the Son of man cometh." Mat 24:42-44 KJV

Jesus is making it clear we need to watch for His return because we do not know when He will appear. Over the years I've seen many date setters, false prophets and end of days timelines predicting the "Rapture" or the return of Christ. They all failed in their predictions, even though there may be some good logic to their reasoning. Man simply doesn't know when Christ will return, which is why we must always be watching and prepared. As a matter of fact, Jesus explains it's precisely when we think not; He will come and those who are unprepared will be taken off guard. Much like a man who is not expecting a thief to break into his house. However, if the good man is watching and paying attention, then it will be impossible for the thief to catch Him unprepared.

"Who then is a faithful and wise servant, whom his lord hath made ruler over his household, to give them meat in due season? Blessed is that servant, whom his lord when he cometh shall find so doing. Verily I say unto you, That he shall make him ruler over all his goods. But and if that evil servant shall say in his heart, My lord delayeth his coming; And shall begin to smite his fellowservants, and to eat and drink with the drunken; The lord of that servant shall come in a day when he looketh not for him, and in an hour that he is not aware of, And shall cut him asunder, and appoint him his portion with the hypocrites: there shall be weeping and gnashing of teeth." Matthew 24:45-47 KJV

When Jesus returns unexpectedly, will He find you being faithful with the work He has entrusted to you? Will you be paying attention and watching for your master? Those who are, will be blessed. However, those who think in their heart our Lord Jesus has delayed His coming, those who go back to walking in the flesh, they will not only be greatly caught off guard by the Savior's return, but their inheritance will be with the hypocrites, not with those who inherit the Kingdom of God.

These are very frightening verses and should be a grave warning to those who approach their walk with God lightly. While we are saved by the grace of God and not the works of the Law, there is still an expectation of walking in faithfulness and obedience to Christ. Your actions matter; in fact, your actions demonstrate what you truly believe. If you believe that Jesus is Lord, then your walk and the fruit of your actions should be proof of that.

LET us not take our relationship with the Creator of all things lightly. May He find us in a state of faithfulness when He returns.

"NOT EVERY ONE THAT SAITH UNTO ME, LORD, LORD, SHALL ENTER INTO THE KINGDOM OF HEAVEN"

DAY 4

In the last chapter, we discussed how your actions matter and how they demonstrate what you truly believe. While you would not likely hear that preached in any church in America today, the scriptures speak for themselves. Even Jesus talked about how people would be known by their "fruit!"

> "Beware of false prophets, which come to you in sheep's clothing, but inwardly they are ravening wolves. Ye shall know them by their fruits. Do men gather grapes of thorns, or figs of thistles? Even so every good tree bringeth forth good fruit; but a corrupt tree bringeth forth evil fruit. A good tree cannot bring forth evil fruit, neither can a corrupt tree bring forth good fruit. Every tree that bringeth not forth good fruit is hewn down, and cast into the fire. Wherefore by their fruits ye shall know them." Matthew 7:15-20 KJV

Please don't think I'm saying the works of the Law save you. Again, it's by grace through faith. What I'm saying is, the proof is in the fruit. What you truly believe will be demonstrated by how you live your life and treat others.

Now, let's look at what I think might be the scariest words Jesus ever spoke. Again, another verse you won't likely hear preached in many American churches. A verse many tries to avoid or misinterpret.

"Not every one that saith unto me, Lord, Lord, shall enter into the kingdom of heaven; but he that doeth the will of my Father which is in heaven. Many will say to me in that day, Lord, Lord, have we not prophesied in thy name? and in thy name have cast out devils? and in thy name done many wonderful works? And then will I profess unto them, I never knew you: depart from me, ye that work iniquity." Matthew 7:21-23 KJV

Let's take another look at the beginning of this passage and see if we can understand what our Lord Jesus is trying to tell us.

"Not every one that saith unto me, Lord, Lord, shall enter into the kingdom of heaven; but he that doeth the will of my Father which is in heaven." Matthew 7:21 KJV

This is simple and easy to understand; however, many try to complicate this passage because it makes them very uncomfortable. Jesus is simply telling us not everyone who calls Him, or acknowledges Him as Lord, will enter into the kingdom of heaven. He even tells us specifically why this is. They don't do the will of the Father whom is in heaven.

Yes, like it or not, your actions matter. Why? Because your actions demonstrate what you truly believe. Obedience is part of the Christian walk, contrary to what many pastors and churches teach today. Jesus Himself tells us, "if ye love me, keep my commandments". John 14:15 KJV

The Apostle John tells us, "for this is the love of God, that we keep his commandments: and his commandments are not grievous." 1 John 5:3 KJV

MAY we never forget our actions matter! Our obedience matters! May it be demonstrated in the way we live our lives.

> "But be ye doers of the word, and not hearers only, deceiving your own selves." James 1:22 KJV

WARNING IN THINKING HE HAS DELAYED IN HIS COMING

DAY 5

I n Luke, chapter 12, Jesus gives us a chilling parable, a warning to those who would think He has delayed in His return and dare to venture back into the world of sin. This is Luke's version of the story we looked at earlier from Matthew, chapter 24. I want to revisit this warning of thinking the Lord has delayed and going back into sin and contrast it with a similar mistake made by the Israelites in the book of Exodus.

"And the Lord said, Who then is that faithful and wise steward, whom his lord shall make ruler over his household, to give them their portion of meat in due season? Blessed is that servant, whom his lord when he cometh shall find so doing. Of a truth I say unto you, that he will make him ruler over all that he hath. But and if that servant say in his heart, My lord delayeth his coming; and shall begin to beat the menservants and maidens, and to eat and drink, and to be drunken; The lord of that servant will come in a day when he looketh not for him, and at an hour when he is not aware, and will cut him in sunder, and will appoint him his portion with the unbelievers." Luke 12:42-46 KJV

What we see in this parable is a grave warning, but also a great promise! To those who would be faithful in doing the Lord's will, to those who are good stewards of what has been entrusted to them, they will be given authority and trusted with all that the Lord has!

However, those who fail to prepare, fail to watch, and return to their sin, thinking to themselves, the Lord has delayed in His return, to them their portion will be with the nonbelievers. Jesus warns the person who is no longer paying attention, no longer being faithful, they will be caught off guard!

> "The lord of that servant will come in a day when he looketh not for him, and at an hour when he is not aware, and will cut him in sunder, and will appoint him his portion with the unbelievers." Luke 12:46 KJV

This is very serious. The consequence of this are grievous and not to be taken lightly. As I continue to say over and over, your actions matter. Your heart towards God and towards His Son, Jesus, matter.

While we might think it is harsh, Jesus would say "will cut him in sunder, and appoint him his portion with the unbelievers." This is not a new attitude. God has always taken great issue with those whom He would call out of the world only for them to return to their wicked ways and reject His promises and ignore His commandments.

We see a parallel in the book of Exodus, chapter 32. Moses has been up on Mount Sinai receiving the Ten Commandments from God. While Moses is communing with the Most High, the Israelites grow impatient and think to themselves, Moses is delaying in his return and must not be coming back. At this point, the Israelites fall back into old habits and return to the ways of the Egyptians and start worshiping a golden calf.

"And when the people saw that Moses delayed coming down out of the mount, the people gathered themselves together unto Aaron, and said unto him, Up, make us gods, which shall go before us; for as for this Moses, the man that brought us up out of the land of Egypt, we wot not what is become of him." Exodus 32:1 KJV

They had seen all that God had done for them, they had seen the plagues of Egypt, they had seen the parting of the Red Sea, and the mana fall from heaven. Yet, how quickly they fall back into unbelief, thinking their master and mediator with God had delayed and may not return at all.

We might be quick to judge the Hebrews, but Jesus reminds us in the parable above to be on guard or this could happen to us. As far as the harsh judgement Jesus warns about, it's nothing new. This is God's attitude towards this kind of behavior. He is the same today, yesterday and always. We can see God's response to the Israelites returning to their "worldly" ways.

"And the Lord said unto Moses, Go, get thee down; for thy people, which thou broughtest out of the land of Egypt, have corrupted themselves: They have turned aside quickly out of the way which I commanded them: they have made them a molten calf, and have worshipped it, and have sacrificed thereunto, and said, These be thy gods, O Israel, which have brought thee up out of the land of

Egypt. And the Lord said unto Moses, I have seen this people, and, behold, it is a stiffnecked people: Now therefore let me alone, that my wrath may wax hot against them, and that I may consume them: and I will make of thee a great nation." Exodus 32:7-10 KJV

God is so angry about this He is ready to annihilate them all and start over with Moses! While God is convinced by Moses to be merciful, there was still a great price to pay for this sin. You should read the whole chapter for yourself to see what happened.

What I want to focus on now is the very end of the chapter.

"And the Lord said unto Moses, Whosoever hath sinned against me, him will I blot out of my book." Exodus 32:33 KJV

This idea of being blotted out of the Book of Life for turning away from the faith should not fall on Christians as a new idea. While it may seem to just be an Old Testament idea, we also see a warning about this from Jesus Christ Himself in a letter to the Church of Sardis. It's the same warning as in the parable. Be watchful! Be ready! If you fail to do so, there is a great consequence to suffer.

"And unto the angel of the church in Sardis write; These things saith he that hath the seven Spirits of God, and the seven stars; I know thy works, that thou hast a name that thou livest, and art dead. Be watchful, and strengthen the things which remain, that are ready to die: for I have not found thy works perfect before God. Remember therefore how thou hast received and heard, and hold fast, and repent. **If therefore thou shalt not watch, I will come on thee as a thief, and thou shalt not know what hour I will come upon thee.** Thou hast a few names even in Sardis which have not defiled their garments; and they shall walk with me in white: for they are worthy. He that overcometh, the same shall be clothed in white raiment; and **I will not blot out his name out of the book of life**, but I will confess his name before my Father, and before his angels." Revelation 3:1-5 KJV

Jesus warns them to repent and be watchful, otherwise they will be caught off guard and He will come like a thief and they will not be ready. We also see Him promise those who overcome, who remain in the faith and repent, will not be blotted out of the Book of Life. So what does that mean for those who do not overcome?

While you may not hear this preached in the modern American Church, these are the words and warnings of Jesus, our Messiah and Master. We should take them very seriously.

L ET us also not fall into the trap of thinking He has delayed or we have plenty of time before His return. He comes quickly and at a time and hour we think not. He has not delayed His return and He could appear in the sky at any moment. The only question is, are we ready and have we prepared ourselves to meet Him?

HIS RETURN WILL BE OBVIOUS

DAY 6

Jesus not only warns us to be watching for His return with great expectation, but He also warns us not to be deceived about His coming. Jesus seemed to be concerned about this issue, as it's His first response to His disciples when they ask about His coming.

"And as he sat upon the mount of Olives, the disciples came unto him privately, saying, Tell us, when shall these things be? and what shall be the sign of thy coming, and of the end of the world? And Jesus answered and said unto them, Take heed that no man deceive you. For many shall come in my name, saying, I am Christ; and shall deceive many." Matthew 24:3-5 KJV

Jesus warns us there will be those who will come in His name and claiming to be Him! However, in the book of Luke, Jesus lets us know something very important about His return.

"And when he was demanded of the Pharisees, when the

kingdom of God should come, he answered them and said, The kingdom of God cometh not with observation: Neither shall they say, Lo here! or, lo there! for, behold, the kingdom of God is within you. And he said unto the disciples, The days will come, when ye shall desire to see one of the days of the Son of man, and ye shall not see it. And they shall say to you, See here; or, see there: go not after them, nor follow them. **For as the lightning, that lighteneth out of the one part under heaven, shineth unto the other part under heaven; so shall also the Son of man be in his day."** Luke 17:20-24 KJV

What does Jesus mean? "For as the lightning, that lighteneth out of the one part under heaven, shineth unto the other part under heaven; so shall also the Son of man be in his day." I believe He is simply telling us not to be deceived. His coming will be painfully obvious! You won't be able to miss it! You won't need to ponder or speculate or go looking around for Him. Don't follow anyone who tells you He is over there or over here. His return will be without question. It will be like lightning going across the sky.

Jesus also seems to bring this idea home once more at the very end of the Gospel of Luke.

"And they answered and said unto him, Where, Lord? And he said unto them, **Wheresoever the body is, thither will the eagles be gathered together."** Luke 17:37 KJV

For years this statement confused me, then one day, it dawned on me.

Here in Indiana, we have these large birds we call buzzards. They are basically vultures. They have big black bodies and a disgusting bald red head. I can't stand them.

They feed on dead animals and road kill. I suppose they are necessary to the ecosystem, but I can't stand them nonetheless. This large bird does something very interesting. It's not uncommon to see three or four of them high in the sky, circling an area, especially over a field, woods or farm. When you see them in the sky, circling an area, you can be sure of one thing. Somewhere in that location is a dead animal! When Jesus makes the strange statement, "**wheresoever the body is, thither will the eagles be gathered together,**" He is using a word picture to demonstrate His return will be very obvious.

MAY we not allow ourselves to be fearful, thinking we might somehow miss His return. Let us not be afraid we won't know or understand it has happened. His return will be so very obvious to His followers. Like lightening flashing from the east to the west, like eagles gathering together, so shall be His return!

JESUS IS RETURNING AS JUDGE AND KING

DAY 7

J esus first came as the Savior of the world. However, when He returns, He will come as King and will judge all according to their works. There will be a great separation of the sheep and the goats. All, both small and great, will bow down before Him and confess He is Lord. The remnant, those who obey the commandments of God and hold the testimony of Jesus Christ, will rejoice and delight in His coming. While the rest of the world will mourn and cry out for the mountains to fall upon them and to hide them from His wrath.

"And the kings of the earth, and the great men, and the rich men, and the chief captains, and the mighty men, and every bondman, and every free man, hid themselves in the dens and in the rocks of the mountains; And said to the mountains and rocks, Fall on us, and hide us from the face of him that sitteth on the throne, and from the wrath of the Lamb: For the great day of his wrath is come; and who shall be able to stand?" Revelation 6:15-17 KJV

We could be the generation who will see the return of Jesus Christ, our Messiah. However, I fear very few are paying attention. Very few are ready to meet Him. Very few are watching and have prepared themselves.

Many are expecting a weak type of Jesus to come. A Jesus who has no regard for sin, who only wants to be our buddy. Having this mindset is a grave mistake. In the Book of Revelation, John describes for us what it is like to stand in the presence of Jesus, our King.

> "And I turned to see the voice that spake with me. And being turned, I saw seven golden candlesticks; And in the midst of the seven candlesticks one like unto the Son of man, clothed with a garment down to the foot, and girt about the paps with a golden girdle. His head and his hairs were white like wool, as white as snow; and his eyes were as a flame of fire; And his feet like unto fine brass, as if they burned in a furnace; and his voice as the sound of many waters. And he had in his right hand seven stars: and out of his mouth went a sharp twoedged sword: and his countenance was as the sun shineth in his strength. And when I saw him, I fell at his feet as dead." Revelation 1:12-17 KJV

Jesus is not our buddy. He is our Lord and Master. Our King and Righteous Judge! When John saw Messiah in all His glory, he fell at His feet as though dead! He did not give Jesus a high five and casually approach Him.

We should be very careful about how we approach our relationship with our Lord. We need to take our walk with Him very seriously. We should start by doing as the scriptures say and examine ourselves daily to make sure we are truly walking in the faith.

"Examine yourselves, whether ye be in the faith; prove your own selves. Know ye not your own selves, how that Jesus Christ is in you, except ye be reprobates?" 2 Corinthians 13:5 KJV

We must practice righteousness and holiness and walk in it daily. We should be growing in righteousness, growing in repentance and growing in our desire for the return of our King. Let us not be fooled. Let us not allow the corrupt and apostate modern church to convince us our actions don't matter! Our behavior is relevant. I believe the Apostle John said it best.

"Little children, let no man deceive you: he that doeth righteousness is righteous, even as he is righteous. He that committeth sin is of the devil; for the devil sinneth from the beginning. For this purpose the Son of God was manifested, that he might destroy the works of the devil." 1 John 3:7-8 KJV

I've said it before, and I'll say it over and over again. Our actions matter. Our actions demonstrate what we truly believe. If we really believe the coming of Messiah is nigh and is at the door, if we believe He is returning as King and will judge all according to their works, then our lives and our walk should reflect this belief. We must ask ourselves and examine ourselves. Do we actually believe this? Are we living in such a way as to be ready for His return? Or, are we more concerned by the trinkets of this world and the lust of the flesh?

"For what is a man profited, if he shall gain the whole world, and lose his own soul? or what shall a man give in exchange for his soul? For the Son of man shall come in the glory of his Father with his angels; **and then he shall reward every man according to his works.**" Matthew 16:26-27 KJV

8

WOE UNTO YOU THAT DESIRE THE DAY OF THE LORD

DAY 8

While we are to be diligently waiting and watching for the Messiah to appear, and to prepare ourselves to meet Him, we must not confuse this with waiting and desiring for God's wrath and judgement to fall upon the earth.

The prophet Amos tells us those who long for the judgement and wrath of God are being very foolish, not understanding what they are asking.

> "Woe unto you that desire the day of the Lord! to what end is it for you? the day of the Lord is darkness, and not light. As if a man did flee from a lion, and a bear met him; or went into the house, and leaned his hand on the wall, and a serpent bit him. Shall not the day of the Lord be darkness, and not light? even very dark, and no brightness in it?" Amos 5:18-20 KJV

Amos is trying to tell us we should not desire such a thing. It is a day, a time, so dark there is no light. No bright spot of hope to be found. It would be as if you escaped the grasp of a lion only to run right into a bear. There is no hope during this time, there is no escaping its darkness.

The day of the Lord is not reserved for God's faithful. It's not for the righteous ones; therefore, why should we desire it? As Amos plainly says, "*to what end is it for you?*"

> "For God hath not appointed us to wrath, but to obtain salvation by our Lord Jesus Christ, Who died for us, that, whether we wake or sleep, we should live together with him." 1 Thessalonians 5:9-10 KJV

While we anticipate the rule and peace of the Messiah to be eternally upon the earth, we should desire mercy, not wrath. We should desire peace, not destruction. For this is the desire of God. He is patient and long-suffering towards sinners, as should be our hearts towards our fellow man. Rather than looking forward to this old world being judged and getting what it deserves, let us pray and hope for revival! Let us pray and hope our enemies might come to know Jesus and be saved from eternal damnation! This is the mind of Christ. Yes, the day is coming when He will judge all the earth. All will stand and give an account before Him. However, until that day, His heart is that we would preach the gospel and bring as many as possible into the Kingdom of God.

We can see this is the Lord's heart from the Gospel of Luke. The disciples wanted to call down fire upon the Samaritans for refusing to receive them. They thought this would please Jesus. However, what they discovered was this is not the mind and spirit of Christ. He desires salvation, not destruction. As should we.

> "And it came to pass, when the time was come that he

should be received up, he stedfastly set his face to go to Jerusalem, And sent messengers before his face: and they went, and entered into a village of the Samaritans, to make ready for him. And they did not receive him, because his face was as though he would go to Jerusalem. And when his disciples James and John saw this, they said, Lord, wilt thou that we command fire to come down from heaven, and consume them, even as Elias did? But he turned, and rebuked them, and said, Ye know not what manner of spirit ye are of. For the Son of man is not come to destroy men's lives, but to save them. And they went to another village." Luke 9:51-56 KJV

9

IT WILL BE LIKE THE DAYS OF NOAH

DAY 9

Jesus tells us His coming will not only be sudden, but it will be unexpected and the world will be oblivious to the urgency that His return is near.

Jesus says people will be doing normal life, things will seem to move forward as they always have. People will be eating, drinking, and getting married.

In the days of Noah, destruction came, and the world was taken completely by surprise. For years, they had ignored the preaching and warnings of Noah. The coming of Christ will be like the flood of Noah. Once it comes, it's too late. Either you're prepared or you're not. Jesus also likens the times to the days of Lot. People were building houses, buying and selling, and planting fields. They were living their life and were unaware trouble was near. Then fire and brimstone rained down upon them all. This is how it will be when the Son of Man is revealed.

"And as it was in the days of Noe, so shall it be also in the days of the Son of man. They did eat, they drank, they

married wives, they were given in marriage, until the day
that Noah entered into the ark, and the flood came, and
destroyed them all. Likewise also as it was in the days of
Lot; they did eat, they drank, they bought, they sold, they
planted, they builded; But the same day that Lot went out
of Sodom it rained fire and brimstone from heaven, and
destroyed them all. Even thus shall it be in the day when
the Son of man is revealed." Luke 17:26-30 KJV

As followers of Christ, we should not be like the world
and be taken off guard! In both scenarios, God's people were
preserved and knew in advance trouble was coming. Noah
obeyed God and built an ark which preserved him and his
family. Lot, his wife, and two of his daughters fled the city
before it rained down fire and brimstone. However, Lot's
wife did not obey the instructions and looked back and she
was turned into a pillar of salt.

We should draw comfort knowing God will preserve us
and protect His own. Like Lot and Noah, we need to be
watching and ready to obey God when the time comes.

We also see a foreshadow of this during the first
Passover. The Israelites were instructed to eat the Passover
with their shoes on and staff in hand. The reason for this is
they needed to be ready to flee Egypt at a moment's notice!

"This is how you are to eat it: with your cloak tucked into
your belt, your sandals on your feet and your staff in your
hand. Eat it in haste; it is the Lord's Passover." Exodus
12:11 KJV

∾

WE SHOULD APPROACH *every day ready and prepared to leave this earth suddenly and without notice. May this urgency be our attitude, our mindset. May we be ready to meet our King in the air, where we shall be forever with Him.*

REMEMBER LOT'S WIFE

DAY 10

J esus tells us His appearing will be like the day of Lot and Noah. People will be doing everyday things like buying, selling, building, planting, getting married, eating and drinking. They will expect nothing to change. The coming of Christ will be a huge surprise to the world. However, it's not to be a huge surprise to us.

Now, it's very possible Jesus was warning His followers of the coming judgement which would come upon Jerusalem in 70 A.D. He tells them when the day comes to flee to the mountains do not bother trying to grab their stuff or return home if they are in the fields working. Either way, this still has great meaning for us today. Especially if we are the generation to witness the return of Christ.

He warns them to remember Lot's wife. While Lot and his two daughters fled the city, his wife disobeyed God's command to not look back, and she was then turned into a pillar of salt! (See Genesis 19:26 KJV)

Likewise, Jesus is warning His followers there is a great cost to pay for desiring the world, for looking back, for trying to preserve your own way of life. This is also true for us today. God may call us to do a great work for the Kingdom of God; He may call us into ministry. We must not dare look back, longing for the days of sin, longing for our old life and lifestyle. Let us not forget, we were purchased with a price and we are no longer our own.

> "In that day, he which shall be upon the housetop, and his stuff in the house, let him not come down to take it away: and he that is in the field, let him likewise not return back. **Remember Lot's wife.** Whosoever shall seek to save his life shall lose it; and whosoever shall lose his life shall preserve it." Luke 17:31-33 KJV

May we march forward in our faith and relationship with Christ. Not with an attitude of self-perseverance, but with an attitude of self-sacrifice for the Kingdom of God.

> "And Jesus said unto him, No man, having put his hand to the plough, and looking back, is fit for the kingdom of God." Luke 9:62 KJV

MAY we not be like the world, oblivious to the coming of Messiah and the coming judgement. Let us not be like Lot's wife, looking backwards. We have a bright future and a whole eternity of peace, grace and love awaiting us. Keep looking forward. Our Master's return is nigh.

A CROWN OF RIGHTEOUSNESS

While it is of the utmost importance to be waiting and watching for Christ with a sense of urgency and expectation, our attitude and posture about His return is equally important and even comes with reward.

Maybe you've heard people say, "Yes, I want the Lord to return, just not yet, I want to see my kids graduate college." "I want to accomplish my career goals first, I want to get married first, I want to have kids first, I want to finish school and accomplish this or that."

You wouldn't find this attitude within Christianity in other parts of the world. After all, many of our brothers and sisters are facing hard times and even persecution for their faith. They would delight in His appearing if it were to happen right now. We should long for His return; we should long to hear the trumpet blast in the sky! Maybe we've gotten a little too comfortable here in the West, especially the United States of America.

Do we really think there is an experience out there in the world which can compete with an eternity with the King

of Kings and Lord of Lords? A worldly and momentary pleasure which can compete with the Savior of our souls and an
eternity of peace, rest and joy? This just shows we are a little
too comfortable in our current lifestyles or we just don't
quite understand what God has in store for those who
love Him.

The scriptures tell us no man has even conceived what
God has waiting for us!

> "But as it is written, Eye hath not seen, nor ear heard,
> neither have entered into the heart of man, the things
> which God hath prepared for them that love him." 1
> Corinthians 2:9 KJV

*WE SHOULD delight in the coming of Messiah! The life He has
prepared for us is so far beyond what we could ever hope or think.
There will even be crowns for those who truly, truly, delight in
Him and His return. I don't know about you, but I want a crown
from the King himself! Not just any crown, but the Crown of
Righteousness which is promised to those who anxiously await
His appearing. Lord, help us not to sacrifice our heavenly
rewards, our heavenly crowns for the unfulfilling and rotting
pleasures of this old world.*

> "Henceforth there is laid up for me a crown of
> righteousness, which the Lord, the righteous judge, shall
> give me at that day: and not to me only, but unto all them
> also that love his appearing." 2 Timothy 4:8 KJV

THE LUKEWARM CHURCH

DAY 12

I n the Book of Revelation, we see Jesus dictate seven letters to seven churches in Asia. The letters appear to be report cards and nearly every church is called to repent and change their current direction or face severe consequences.

I happen to believe these warnings go far beyond just those seven literal churches. I believe those seven churches are also types of churches in the world we might be a part of right now; but also, I believe they represent the church ages throughout history.

With that being said, I think we are living in the last church age, the Laodicean Church, also known as the luke-warm church. This should give us cause to pause and examine ourselves!

This particular church had need of nothing. They had plenty of clothes, they had shelter, they had food; and because of their comfort, they couldn't comprehend how desperate their need was for Jesus. Even more frightening, they didn't seem to understand they didn't really have Jesus. What they had was religion and the pleasures of this world.

It pains me to say it, but this sums up a majority of the believers I know today. Even myself, if I'm being honest and looking in the mirror, could fall into this category. This is the modern Christian Church, at least here in the western part of the world.

Jesus warns He will have no part of this church. Either you will be on fire for Him or not. He's not interested in wishy-washy followers. He desires we be hot in our faith, not lukewarm. He even says He would prefer you were just flat-out cold in your relationship with Him rather than be lukewarm.

Have you ever taken a drink of tea or coffee only to remember it has set for an hour? It tastes awful; you just want to spit it back out into the cup or sink. That's how Jesus feels about lukewarm faith.

"And unto the angel of the church of the Laodiceans write; These things saith the Amen, the faithful and true witness, the beginning of the creation of God; **I know thy works, that thou art neither cold nor hot: I would thou wert cold or hot. So then because thou art lukewarm, and neither cold nor hot, I will spue thee out of my mouth.** Because thou sayest, I am rich, and increased with goods, and have need of nothing; and knowest not that thou art wretched, and miserable, and poor, and blind, and naked: I counsel thee to buy of me gold tried in the fire, that thou mayest be rich; and white raiment, that thou mayest be clothed, and that the shame of thy nakedness do not appear; and anoint thine eyes with eyesalve, that thou mayest see." Revelation 3:14-18 KJV

Jesus tells the Laodicean Church, in spite of them having the things of this world in abundance, they are in fact not rich. Instead, He tells them they are wretched, miserable, poor, blind, and naked!

Without an intimate relationship with Christ, we have nothing. The modern Western Church is blinded by their wealth and their comfort. So much so, they can't even see they don't really have Christ in their lives.

However, Jesus loves us so much He is standing outside the door of the church, wanting to come in, wanting to have a real relationship with us. If only we would repent and hear His voice.

LET us overcome this sin of lukewarmness. Let us open the door and dine with the King. May we be on fire for Christ every day of our lives and may we never fall into the wretched state of indifference.

"As many as I love, I rebuke and chasten: be zealous therefore, and repent. Behold, I stand at the door, and knock: if any man hear my voice, and open the door, I will come in to him, and will sup with him, and he with me. To him that overcometh will I grant to sit with me in my throne, even as I also overcame, and am set down with my Father in his throne. He that hath an ear, let him hear what the Spirit saith unto the churches." Revelation 3:19-22 KJV

13

GENETIC MODIFICATION AND ARTIFICIAL INTELLIGENCE IN THE LAST DAYS

DAY 13

To some, the idea of genetically modified humans might seem completely outlandish. But, to those who have studied in depth the days of Noah and are paying attention to current trends, this has been a long time coming.

Our media and technology industries continue to report and boast about developments in genetics. Even more so, they are demonstrating their ability to not only genetically modify humans, but to merge them with artificial intelligence. These are some interesting, albeit scary times, we are living in.

I've told my podcast listening audience for years, "In your lifetime, you're going to see non-human individuals walking around." I'm referring to people who have either been genetically altered from God's original design, or people who have merged physically with some kind of artificial intelligence.

Honestly, we shouldn't be shocked by this concept. After all, we have genetically modified animals, plants, and food which is now part of our everyday life. It has been this way for many years. In fact, if you're trying to eat clean, natural, unaltered, non-GMO food here in the United States, then you are going to have to go to a health specialty market and it's going to be expensive. Why? Because there just isn't much food left in the food supply which hasn't been tampered with!

Not only is society screaming to us this is coming, but the scriptures also tell us to be expecting this. The prophet Daniel, when describing the coming world kingdoms, tells us something very interesting about the last kingdom.

> "And whereas thou sawest iron mixed with miry clay, **they shall mingle themselves with the seed of men**: but they shall not cleave one to another, even as iron is not mixed with clay." Daniel 2:43 KJV

They shall mingle themselves with the seed of men? I don't know about you, but this sounds like the manipulation of a human being. It could be a form of genetic modification or maybe the merging of man with artificial intelligence. Either way, Daniel tells us it's not going to go well and they will not cleave to one another.

Another interesting passage which lends itself to this thinking comes from the Apocrypha, which was included in the King James Bible from 1611 through most of the 1800s, before being suspiciously removed. I have an old King James Bible in my library from the 1800s. It once belonged to a church in New York. As did most Bibles from this time, it has the Apocryphal text included in it.

I'm referring to the Apocryphal Book 2nd Esdras. A book filled with very interesting and prophetical text. However, there is one particular verse which always jumps out at me and causes me to pause and think.

"There shall be a confusion also in many places, and the fire shall be oft sent out again, and the wild beasts shall change their places, **and menstruous women shall bring forth monsters.**" 2 Esdras 5:8 KJV

ALSO IN 2ND ESDRAS, we read,

"And the children of a year old shall speak with their voices, the women with child shall bring forth untimely children of three or four months old, and they shall live, and be raised up." 2 Esdras 6:21 KJV

Woman shall bring forth monsters? Children will live being born as early as three months, and will talk?

I wouldn't be surprised if in the next few years or maybe even sooner, we see it normalized for parents to have their babies genetically altered before birth. Society may spin it as a good thing and a way for children to be born free of disease. Parents will try to pick what color eyes their child would have, or how tall, intelligent, athletic or artistic they might be.

However, if we take the time to study what happened during the days of Noah, if we study the apocryphal text, then we will see tampering with God's creation leads to horrific events, followed by great judgement.

I believe genetic modification and artificial intelligence will play a huge role in these last days, and we better pay attention to these trends. Not only pay attention, but more importantly, avoid being a part of it!

May God give us wisdom and have mercy on our souls.

14

THE MARK OF THE BEAST

DAY 14

hen it comes to the mark of the beast described in the Book of Revelation, there have been a lot of opinions and thoughts shared by prophecy lovers throughout the ages. It's no different today, and I certainly have some interesting thoughts on the subject, especially considering the world we are living in today. A world where people at this very moment in history are getting microchips in their hands and soon in their heads.

We are told in the Book of Revelation, the false prophet will come on the scene and will cause many to make an image to the beast and worship this image. They will also get his mark in their hands or foreheads. Without this mark, we cannot buy or sell.

> "And he causeth all, both small and great, rich and poor, free and bond, to receive a mark in their right hand, or in their foreheads: And that no man might buy or sell, save he that had the mark, or the name of the beast, or the number of his name." Revelation 13:16-17 KJV

Many, including myself, believe this is likely two-fold. You have an allegiance to the beast system, and there is a microchip of some sort associated with the mark. This mark holds all your financial, and maybe even personal, information. This makes perfect sense, and it's an effective way to control the population. If you step out of line, those in power could simply turn off your accounts via the microchip, making it very difficult for survival. Same goes for those who refuse to take the mark; they would be essentially alienated from society and unable to take part in commerce. Therein lies the temptation. It will be very difficult to refuse the mark when you or the people you love are hungry and in need.

We must settle this in our hearts now! Should this time come upon us, we must have already decided, no matter what, we will not take the mark!

The scriptures make it very clear, those who take the mark will be lost forever. There will be no salvation, no redemption for those who have worshiped the image of the beast and taken his mark. They will be tormented for all eternity.

> "And the smoke of their torment ascendeth up for ever and ever: and they have no rest day nor night, **who worship the beast and his image, and whosoever receiveth the mark of his name.**" Revelation 14:11 KJV

Because there is no salvation or mercy found for those who take the mark, I am therefore led to believe there is more than just a chip and allegiance to the beast involved. It could be there is also a genetic alteration component to the mark.

We know from reading ancient Dead Sea Scrolls, such as

the Book of Enoch, the Book of Jubilees and others, there was no salvation available for the Nephilim. These Nephilim, or giants, came to be on the earth through an incidence where the Watchers, the Sons of God, left their heavenly habitation and had sexual relations with earthly women. To understand this more, you need to start by studying Genesis, chapter 6. I would also recommend studying 2nd Peter and the Book of Jude.

> "And the angels which kept not their first estate, but left their own habitation, he hath reserved in everlasting chains under darkness unto the judgment of the great day." Jude 1:6 KJV

WE ARE LIVING in some very interesting and strange times. It's possible God has chosen us to be the generation who would see these very things develop, but more importantly, see the return of our Messiah and Savior, Jesus Christ.

Let us not only prepare to meet Him, but let us prepare our hearts and minds to deal with these strange developments which are quickly coming upon the earth.

15

WE ARE NOT APPOINTED TO GOD'S WRATH

DAY 15

J udgement is coming quickly upon this sinful world. It is coming suddenly as a thief in the night. However, we must not live in fear of this wrath if we know the Savior, Jesus Christ. For as the scriptures declare, we are not appointed to God's wrath.

"Therefore let us not sleep, as do others; but let us watch and be sober. For they that sleep sleep in the night; and they that be drunken are drunken in the night. But let us, who are of the day, be sober, putting on the breastplate of faith and love; and for an helmet, the hope of salvation. **For God hath not appointed us to wrath,** but to obtain salvation by our Lord Jesus Christ, Who died for us, that, whether we wake or sleep, we should live together with him." 1 Thessalonians 5:6-10 KJV

Again, we see this language about not falling asleep. The wrath of God will take the whole earth by surprise because they are asleep, unaware, and drunk. But those of us who belong to the Savior are set apart. We are not to be like the rest of the world. We are to be sober, awake and paying attention, so the day does not take us by surprise.

While we are not appointed to wrath, we still have a responsibility to be paying attention and to be walking in God's ways and in His favor. I'll say it once again. Our actions matter! Why? Because they demonstrate what we truly believe.

Let's also look at what the prophet Isaiah said about God's wrath as it pertains to His chosen.

"Come, my people, enter thou into thy chambers, and shut thy doors about thee: hide thyself as it were for a little moment, until the indignation be overpast. For, behold, the Lord cometh out of his place to punish the inhabitants of the earth for their iniquity: the earth also shall disclose her blood, and shall no more cover her slain." Isaiah 26:20-21 KJV

Again, we see a picture of God's people being preserved, being protected and spared from the wrath to come. However, we are told to enter our chambers, suggesting there is at least some action, some responsibility required on our part. I believe this action is faith. We must believe and trust in God and in His Son, Jesus. Trust He will fulfill His promises to protect and preserve us from His wrath, which will be poured out on all those who dwell on the earth.

LET us not live in fear of the coming day of judgement, but with all soberness, let us be a people who are watching, waiting, trusting and believing on the promises of the King.

16

ONCE HE RETURNS, THERE NO LONGER REMAINS A CHANCE FOR REPENTANCE

DAY 16

We need to understand the seriousness of our relationship with God and His Son, Jesus. So many people believe, but refuse to commit. They want the salvation which comes by knowing Jesus, but they are not interested in the life changes which come along with it. They want all the benefits, but none of the change or responsibility. One day, and I believe soon, our Messiah will appear in the sky, with a great shout! When this happens, it's too late for those who have not trusted in Him and not walked in His ways.

The Bible tells us not to delay in this decision. After all, tomorrow is promised to no one. We could die or He could appear. Either way, the result is the same; an eternity separated from God, suffering in the lake of fire, unless you have salvation which only comes by an intimate relationship with Jesus Christ.

"For he saith, I have heard thee in a time accepted, and in the day of salvation have I succoured thee: behold, now is

the accepted time; behold, now is the day of salvation."
2nd Corinthians 6:2 KJV

I fear so many are giving up their eternal inheritance, and for what? Momentary pleasures? I'm reminded of Esau who sold his birthright to Jacob for a bowl of soup. He gave it all up, his entire inheritance, to feed his flesh. When the time came for the blessing to be given, it was too late for Esau. Though he begged his father Issac, nothing could be done. He had given up his inheritance, he had traded it for worldly pleasures. Oh Lord, help us to not be so foolish as Esau! Help us to fear You and walk in Your ways. Help us to have faith and believe upon Your only begotten Son!

"Follow peace with all men, and holiness, without which no man shall see the Lord: Looking diligently lest any man fail of the grace of God; lest any root of bitterness springing up trouble you, and thereby many be defiled; Lest there be any fornicator, or profane person, as Esau, who for one morsel of meat sold his birthright. **For ye know how that afterward, when he would have inherited the blessing, he was rejected: for he found no place of repentance, though he sought it carefully with tears.**" Hebrews 12:14-17 KJV

LET us not be a profane and foolish people, such as Esau. May the Spirit of God be our guide and may we strive to walk in righteousness, holiness and faith. Don't ignore His voice! Once judgement arrives, it's too late for the lost. Today is the day of salvation.

17

WATCH AND PRAY ALWAYS TO BE FOUND WORTHY TO ESCAPE

DAY 17

In the Gospel of Luke, Jesus tells the parable of the fig tree. What we learn from this parable is, if we are paying attention, if we are watching as commanded, then we shall see the day of judgement approaching. Therefore, we should be ready for it; it should not take us by surprise.

> "And he spake to them a parable; Behold the fig tree, and all the trees; When they now shoot forth, ye see and know of your own selves that summer is now nigh at hand. So likewise ye, when ye see these things come to pass, know ye that the kingdom of God is nigh at hand." Luke 21:29-31 KJV

Now there is no doubt Jesus is talking to His followers about the coming judgement on Jerusalem which came in 70 A.D. He even tells them their generation will not pass away until all these things come to pass.

"Verily I say unto you, This generation shall not pass away, till all be fulfilled." Luke 21:32 KJV

However, we must always remember the scriptures can have multiple meanings and multiple fulfillments. This is most assuredly a word for us today. Like the disciples of Jesus, we can learn from the fig tree. When we see the End Times approaching, as we do now, we too know the end is near. Therefore, the coming of the Son of Man must be on the horizon and the Kingdom of God is at hand!

Jesus warns His followers to be careful about being distracted by the trinkets of this world. He warns about the dangers of taking their eyes off Him and failing to pay attention. As we have already discussed, when we fail to watch, we set ourselves up to be taken by surprise, and judgement will come when we least expect it.

But, if we are not appointed to God's wrath, why then should we worry about being taken by surprise?

We have a responsibility and our actions matter. If we take our eyes off of Jesus, if we ignore the season we are living in, we might find ourselves falling into sin and backsliding into the lust of the flesh. If so, and the Master returns while we are in this state of rebellion, our portion will be with the unbelievers! (See Luke 12:46 KJV)

Instead, Jesus commands us to be awake, sober, and to be in prayer. Not just any prayer, but a very specific prayer.

"And take heed to yourselves, lest at any time your hearts be overcharged with surfeiting, and drunkenness, and cares of this life, and so that day come upon you unawares. For as a snare shall it come on all them that dwell on the face of the whole earth. **Watch ye therefore, and pray always, that ye may be accounted worthy to escape all**

these things that shall come to pass, and to stand before the Son of man." Luke 29:34-36 KJV

We are told to watch and to be in continuous prayer. Pray we might be counted worthy to escape all these things and to stand before the Son of Man.

Oh, may the following prayer be in our minds, in our hearts, and on our lips every morning!

Lord God Almighty, have mercy on us. May You find us worthy to escape all the judgement and all the tribulation coming upon this fallen world. May we escape it all and stand before the King of Kings, the Lords of Lords, Jesus the Messiah. Amen.

18

IN THE LAST DAYS, SCOFFERS WILL COME

DAY 18

Have you ever told someone, "I think we are living in the last days," only to have them respond with a scoff? One of the responses I have often received over the years is, "Well, people have always thought we were living in the last days."

When someone says something like this to me, I instantly get confirmation we are in fact living in the last days. Why? Because their very response is a fulfillment of prophecy!

> "knowing this first, that there shall come in the last days scoffers, walking after their own lusts, And saying, **Where is the promise of his coming?** For since the fathers fell asleep, all things continue as they were from the beginning of the creation." 2 Peter 3:3-4 KJV

Peter is telling us as the end of days draws near, people will walk in disbelief about it. However, there appears to be a reason for their disbelief. Deep down, they simply don't want to believe it.

Now this should seem strange our brothers and sisters in Christ, the people we go to church with, would not want to see the return of our beloved Messiah. However, in my experience, this seems to be the case. Like it or not, the church has become very lukewarm. They've become very comfortable with their personal lives, which is also a fulfillment of prophecy.

Peter tells us they will scoff because they are walking after their own lust. You see, most people love the world. Even those who claim to be followers of Jesus love the world and their part in it. Therefore, the idea of it coming to an end is a devastating thought for them. This is why you may have heard other Christians say something like the following, "I want Jesus to return, just not yet." They want to see their kids graduate first, or want to accomplish a certain goal first. There is nothing wrong with wanting to see your kids graduate and accomplish certain goals. However, there is an issue with desiring those dreams and other worldly things more than the Kingdom of God, or Christ returning and reigning here on earth.

MAY we not be like the lukewarm scoffers, walking after our own lust and being ignorant of the times we are living in. May we not be so foolish in thinking things continue now as they have from the beginning of creation. Jesus is coming soon and with Him all His promises.

We believe we are in the last days because we see all the surrounding signs. These are the times many believers before us have longed to see. May we embrace it and delight in His approaching return!

19

SEPARATION OF THE SHEEP AND GOATS

DAY 19

I n the book of Matthew, Jesus describes His coming. When He arrives in glory, there will be a great separation of what He calls the sheep and the goats.

All the nations will be gathered before Him to be judged. He will place the sheep at His right hand and the goats at His left hand. The sheep will enter into the kingdom prepared for them, but the goats will enter into everlasting fire prepared for the devil and his angels.

Now, what's most interesting is the conditions of the judgement. Jesus plainly tells us what separated the two groups, and it's not what one might think. The difference between them is the love and charity shown to Christ, through the love and charity shown to those in need. Charity! Jesus tells us, the love and charity we show to those in need is the same as showing those mercies unto Him. Likewise, the lack of love and charity shown to those in need, is as if we didn't extend those mercies and grace to Him.

Open up your hearts because this is so very important for us to understand. If we do not show mercy, if we do not show grace, if we ignore the poor and the needy, then we can expect the same treatment come judgement day.

"Blessed are the merciful: for they shall obtain mercy."
Matthew 5:7 KJV

Let's take a closer look at the words of Jesus in regard to the separation of the sheep and the goats. As we read it, let us reflect on our own lives and see which of the two camps we would fall into today if Jesus appeared right now and gathered the nations to Himself.

"When the Son of man shall come in his glory, and all the holy angels with him, then shall he sit upon the throne of his glory: And before him shall be gathered all nations: and he shall separate them one from another, as a shepherd divideth his sheep from the goats: And he shall set the sheep on his right hand, but the goats on the left. Then shall the King say unto them on his right hand, Come, ye blessed of my Father, inherit the kingdom prepared for you from the foundation of the world: For I was an hungred, and ye gave me meat: I was thirsty, and ye gave me drink: I was a stranger, and ye took me in: Naked, and ye clothed me: I was sick, and ye visited me: I was in prison, and ye came unto me. Then shall the righteous answer him, saying, Lord, when saw we thee an hungred, and fed thee? or thirsty, and gave thee drink? When saw we thee a stranger, and took thee in? or naked, and clothed thee? Or when saw we thee sick, or in prison, and came unto thee? And the King shall answer and say unto them, **Verily I say unto you, Inasmuch as ye have done it unto one of the least of these my brethren, ye have done it**

unto me. Then shall he say also unto them on the left hand, Depart from me, ye cursed, into everlasting fire, prepared for the devil and his angels: For I was an hungred, and ye gave me no meat: I was thirsty, and ye gave me no drink: I was a stranger, and ye took me not in: naked, and ye clothed me not: sick, and in prison, and ye visited me not. Then shall they also answer him, saying, Lord, when saw we thee an hungred, or athirst, or a stranger, or naked, or sick, or in prison, and did not minister unto thee? Then shall he answer them, saying, **Verily I say unto you, Inasmuch as ye did it not to one of the least of these, ye did it not to me.** And these shall go away into everlasting punishment: but the righteous into life eternal." Matthew 25:31-46 KJV

Christ is very clear about how to treat and love those in need, especially our own brothers and sisters in the faith. It matters, and it matters greatly! It's not just a recommendation on our part, but a commandment from Christ. In fact, He claims it is the greatest commandment. If we fail to care for those who need us, it is the same as if we ignored the very needs of Jesus Himself. With this decision, comes a grave judgement.

You see, your actions matter, because your actions demonstrate what you truly believe and who you truly are. Are you a sheep or a goat?

～

MAY we have charity in our hearts, may we always err on the side of grace and mercy. May we always live by the golden rule, to do unto others as we would have done to ourselves.

"But the end of all things is at hand: be ye therefore sober, and watch unto prayer. And above all things have fervent charity among yourselves: for charity shall cover the multitude of sins." I Peter 4:7-8 KJV

20

IN THE LAST DAYS, LOVE AND WISDOM SHALL FLEE FROM THE EARTH

DAY 20

The scriptures describe the end of days as a time when there will be a lack of love for one another, a time where intelligence and wisdom will flee and not be found. A time when people are easily and quickly offended, a time when the only love a person has is a disturbing love for one's self.

Does this sound familiar? To me, this sounds exactly like the world we are living in right now. Truth be told, people have become filled with anger and hate as opposed to love and patience.

Just the other day, I was driving to Indianapolis and while I was stopped at a traffic light, I saw a man get out of his car and start threatening the man in the car next to him. It was completely absurd. People literately have no love for one another and are so easily upset, so easily offended.

"And then shall many be offended, and shall betray one another, **and shall hate one another**. And many false prophets shall rise, and shall deceive many. And because

iniquity shall abound, **the love of many shall wax cold.**"
Matthew 24:10-12 KJV

Are we not seeing this happen in our day?

THERE IS SO much hate for one another and love has
certainty waxed cold. People seem to be out of their minds
and completely irrational in their decision making. They
can't be reasoned with. All they seem to be able to do is get
angry and regurgitate whatever they are hearing coming
through the propaganda box known as the television. Not
only has the love of many waxed cold, not only are people
quickly and easily offended, but quite frankly, intelligence
has fled and is difficult to find.

> "And salt waters shall be found in the sweet, and all
> friends shall destroy one another; then **shall wit hide
> itself**, and **understanding withdraw itself into his secret
> chamber**. And shall be sought of many, and yet not be
> found: then shall unrighteousness and incontinency be
> multiplied upon earth." 2nd Esdras 5:9-10 KJV 1611

*LET us not be like the world, filled with hate and ignorance.
Instead, let us be filled with love and wisdom given to us by the
Holy Spirit. Let us resist the temptation to lash out, go into rages,
and find ourselves so easily offended. Instead, let us demonstrate
restraint and self-control and change the world by showing the
love of Christ to our fellow man.*

21

COME OUT OF HER MY PEOPLE!

DAY 21

I n the Book of Revelation we read about Mystery Babylon, a city who has rejected Christ and become a place of apostasy and wickedness. Over the years, I've held many views on Mystery Babylon and for the longest time I thought it was referring to the United States of America. I may yet be right about this assumption. America is definitely a type and shadow of Babylon in these last days and very well might be the final version we see in the Book of Revelation.

TIME WILL TELL.

However, after years of study and prayer, I have come to believe Mystery Babylon COULD be the great city of Jerusalem, the great city which was judged for their rejection of the Messiah.

Unpacking all of this would require an entire other book; however, let us look at one of many possible reasons to believe this. In the Gospels, before Jesus is arrested, He laments and mourns over Jerusalem. He knows the decisions they have made and will make concerning Himself and the judgement which must come to them as a result.

> "O Jerusalem, Jerusalem, which killest the prophets, and stonest them that are sent unto thee; how often would I have gathered thy children together, as a hen doth gather her brood under her wings, and ye would not! Behold, your house is left unto you desolate: and verily I say unto you, Ye shall not see me, until the time come when ye shall say, Blessed is he that cometh in the name of the Lord."
> Luke 13:34-35 KJV

Over and over, God has shown mercy to Israel by sending prophets to warn them. Yet, over and over, they reject these prophets and even kill them, including the greatest prophet, the Messiah, our Lord Jesus Christ. As a result, great and horrible judgement came to Jerusalem in 70 A.D. where potentially a million Jews were slaughtered and the city was burned to the ground. Not just the city, but the Holy Temple was torn down and not a single stone left upon another, as Jesus foretold in the Gospels.

> "And Jesus said unto them, See ye not all these things? verily I say unto you, There shall not be left here one stone upon another, that shall not be thrown down." Matthew 24:2 KJV

We see similar language used in the description of Mystery Babylon regarding the prophets of God.

> "And in her was found the blood of prophets, and of saints, and of all that were slain upon the earth."
> Revelation 18:24 KJV

Mystery Babylon is guilty of the same crimes Jesus proclaimed about Jerusalem in the Gospels. The Book of Revelation also makes another claim against Jerusalem and it is often ignored by modern day prophecy teachers.

"And when they shall have finished their testimony, the beast that ascendeth out of the bottomless pit shall make war against them, and shall overcome them, and kill them. And their dead bodies shall lie in **the street of the great city, which spiritually is called Sodom and Egypt,** where also our Lord was crucified." Revelation 11:7-8 KJV

The prophecy is telling us Jerusalem has become, in a spiritual sense, the same as Sodom and Egypt. Just as both of those nations were judged for their great wickedness, so too was Jerusalem.

Again, we would need an entire book or documentary to unpack all of this. We are just scratching the surface at the moment.

Regardless of who Mystery Babylon is, whether it be Jerusalem, Rome, or the United States of America, the most important thing for us to do is to come out from among her as God commands it.

"And I heard another voice from heaven, saying, **Come out of her, my people, that ye be not partakers of her sins, and that ye receive not of her plagues.** For her sins have reached unto heaven, and God hath remembered her iniquities." Revelation 18:4-5 KJV

It is possible this was a warning to God's children to flee the city of Jerusalem in 70 A.D., much like Lot was commanded to flee to the mountains and hurry himself and his family out of Sodom, lest they be destroyed in the judgement. This could also be a future warning to the great city of Jerusalem, or maybe even a Babylonian-style nation such as the United States of America.

This may also be a spiritual warning for us today. After all, we live in a modern day Babylonian society and we need not be partakers of the wickedness.

So many Christians look, talk, and walk just like the nonbeliever. Watching the same wicked television shows, listening to the same filthy music, taking part in the same ungodly activities. This should not be so, and judgement could very well be right around the corner. We need to come out of Babylon and be set apart!

MAY we take up our cross and be salt and light to this dying world. Let us spiritually come out of Babylon, lest we be destroyed with her. May we also be willing to literally and physically come out of Babylon if we are called to do so by our Lord.

22

O LORD, HOW LONG SHALL I CRY?

DAY 22

As the people of God, we are sojourners in a foreign land while we are on this earth. We are surrounded by things we don't want to be surrounded by. We see things we don't want to see and our souls can be very much vexed by the sin and godlessness all around us every day. This is especially true in these last days. You can't even walk through a shopping mall or watch daytime television without some form of perversion, without some kind of temptation calling out to you. This is a very hard time for those who desire to walk in righteousness and holiness.

I'm reminded of the prophet Habakkuk, who in his day, was dealing with something very similar to what we are dealing with now.

> "The burden which Habakkuk the prophet did see. O Lord, how long shall I cry, and thou wilt not hear! Even cry out unto thee of violence, and thou wilt not save! Why dost thou shew me iniquity, and cause me to behold grievance? For spoiling and violence are before me: and

there are that raise up strife and contention. Therefore the
law is slacked, and judgment doth never go forth: for the
wicked doth compass about the righteous; therefore
wrong judgment proceedeth." Habakkuk 1:1-4 KJV

Habakkuk is complaining to God about the wickedness
which seems to go on day in and day out without being
checked or limited. There is no right judgement, and no one
cares any longer for God's laws. Habakkuk is questioning,
and crying out to God, how long! He is wondering how
much longer God will turn a blind eye to all this evil.

It's a valid question, and a question we might ask God in
our day. There was a time when America might have been
associated with righteousness. Right judgement went forth
and a majority of people were good and polite. There was a
time when our culture revered the ways of God and
followed diligently the teachings of the Savior, Jesus Christ.
These teachings were even taught to our children in public
school and was the foundational belief of even our most
prestige universities.

Now the very opposite is true. America has lost its way
and it would appear America is not alone in this, but the
whole world is now heading toward this trend. There is a
growing hatred and disdain towards God and God's people.
We have become like Habakkuk in his day, surrounded by
evil, wondering, how long will God permit things to go on
like this?

The good news is God does give an answer to Habakkuk,
and it's one of my favorite responses in all the Bible. It's a
response I keep near and dear to my heart.

"Behold ye among the heathen, and regard, and wonder

marvelously: for I will work a work in your days which ye will not believe, though it be told you." Habakkuk 1:5 KJV

God is telling Habakkuk, He is in fact paying attention and He is about to do something. It will be so incredible, mind-blowing, marvelous, and amazing. However, God can't even tell Habakkuk about it, because frankly, Habakkuk wouldn't even be able to believe it!

Sometimes we make the mistake of thinking God has taken a step back and is no longer paying attention, no longer working in our days. This couldn't be farther from the truth. God is very involved in these last days. He's watching, He's working, and He just might do something so amazing and marvelous we wouldn't believe it even if it be told to us in advance.

MAY we pray the prayer of Habakkuk, asking God to do great and marvelous works in our days. We have read about His greatness; we have heard the ancient stories. May we now be witnesses to even greater works here in our generation, in these very last days. Amen.

"O Lord, I have heard thy speech, and was afraid: O Lord, revive thy work in the midst of the years, in the midst of the years make known; in wrath remember mercy." Habakkuk 3:2 KJV

23

THE LORD KNOWS HOW TO DELIVER THE GODLY

DAY 23

Jesus tells us His return and judgement will come during a time similar to the days of Lot and Noah.

"And as it was in the days of Noe, so shall it be also in the days of the Son of man. They did eat, they drank, they married wives, they were given in marriage, until the day that Noah entered into the ark, and the flood came, and destroyed them all. **Likewise also as it was in the days of Lot; they did eat, they drank, they bought, they sold, they planted, they builded; But the same day that Lot went out of Sodom it rained fire and brimstone from heaven, and destroyed them all. Even thus shall it be in the day when the Son of man is revealed.**" Luke 17:26-30 KJV

I believe the above words are a loaded statement, and it may have a double meaning or fulfillment. On one hand, our Messiah is warning Jerusalem His judgement will come sudden and unexpected, as it did in 70 A.D.

On the other hand, He could be describing what it will be like at the very end of days, just before His Second Coming. If this is true, then His coming must be near, at the door. After all, are we not living in the days of Lot? America, and really the entire world, have become much like Sodom. We are told in the scriptures the destruction of Sodom is to be an example of what would come to those who would live ungodly.

"For if God spared not the angels that sinned, but cast them down to hell, and delivered them into chains of darkness, to be reserved unto judgment; And spared not the old world, but saved Noah the eighth person, a preacher of righteousness, bringing in the flood upon the world of the ungodly; **And turning the cities of Sodom and Gomorrha into ashes condemned them with an overthrow, making them an ensample unto those that after should live ungodly.**" 2 Peter 2:4-6 KJV

This should cause us to shutter! Sometimes I feel we may have even surpassed the wickedness of Sodom. Especially as we continue to push ungodly and filthy boundaries. How much longer can God withhold His overdue judgement? How much longer will God tolerate our filth and perversions?

However, the scriptures give us some much needed and encouraging information. God reminds us, even in the mist of great judgement, He knows how to protect and preserve His own! We must remember, before the flood, God preserved Noah and his family. Before the fire rained down on Sodom, God sent holy messengers to escort Lot and his family out of the city. While judgement is most definitely around the corner, and must certainly come, those walking in the ways of YAH, who have the testimony of Jesus Christ and obey the commandments of God, need not be afraid!

Let's continue reading from 2nd Peter.

> "And delivered just Lot, vexed with the filthy conversation of the wicked: (For that righteous man dwelling among them, in seeing and hearing, vexed his righteous soul from day to day with their unlawful deeds;) **The Lord knoweth how to deliver the godly out of temptations, and to reserve the unjust unto the day of judgment to be punished.**" 2 Peter 2:7-9 KJV

LET us walk closely with the Lord of Lords and King of Kings. May we put our trust and hope in His great love and protection. Let us not live and walk in fear of the troubles, tribulations and judgements coming quickly upon the earth.

"Peace I leave with you, my peace I give unto you: not as the world giveth, give I unto you. Let not your heart be troubled, neither let it be afraid." John 14:27 KJV

24

THE PATIENCE OF THE SAINTS

DAY 24

In the Book of Revelation, we see a letter written to the Church of Philadelphia. This seems to be the only church which doesn't receive correction or a rebuke. Rather, they are praised for their willingness to suffer and keep the word of the Messiah.

Although they are worn down by the world and have very little strength left, they continue to persevere in the faith and have not denied His name. As a result, they receive a great blessing on account of it.

Their enemies will be put under their feet and this will be done in a way which allows the entire world know they are loved by the Messiah. Because of their faithfulness, they will be spared from the temptation which is coming upon all who dwell on the earth.

"And to the angel of the church in Philadelphia write; These things saith he that is holy, he that is true, he that hath the key of David, he that openeth, and no man shutteth; and shutteth, and no man openeth; I know thy works: behold, I have set before thee an open door, and no man can shut it: for thou hast a little strength, and hast kept my word, and hast not denied my name. Behold, I will make them of the synagogue of Satan, which say they are Jews, and are not, but do lie; behold, I will make them to come and worship before thy feet, and to know that I have loved thee. **Because thou hast kept the word of my patience, I also will keep thee from the hour of temptation, which shall come upon all the world, to try them that dwell upon the earth."** Revelation 3:7-10 KJV

As we move into the end of days, we should seek to be like those of the Church of Philadelphia. We should be saints who have settled it in their hearts to walk out the great faith and to obey the commandments of God. Also, being saints who have resolved to persevere in the face of trials and persecutions and who refuse to deny the name of Jesus.

Trouble may be on the horizon for believers in these last days. In fact, persecution of Christians around the world is at an all-time high, at least in our recent history. I wonder, who is a faithful and wise servant? Who, by action and faith, live according to God's commandments and the words of Christ? We should all examine ourselves, take a long look in the mirror, and work out our salvation with fear and trembling. (See Philippians 2:12 KJV)

∾

OUR ACTIONS MATTER. They matter because they demonstrate what we truly believe. The Church of Philadelphia didn't just keep the faith. They also walked it out with their actions and

therefore found themselves being praised, encouraged and protected by the Messiah.

"Here is the patience of the saints: **here are they that keep the commandments of God, and the faith of Jesus.**" Revelation 14:12 KJV

25

THE SPIRIT OF JEZEBEL - PART 1

DAY 25

Right now, one of the most destructive, harmful, faith-crippling and life-destroying movements taking place in the world is what I like to call "the spirit of Jezebel." When I say the spirit of Jezebel, I am mostly referring to sexual immorality. However, there are other aspects we don't have time to address in this book.

This spirit is not only vexing the souls of men, but in today's culture it is just as harmful, if not even more harmful, to women. Not only are women indulging in pornography in staggering numbers, but women are also indulging in overall sexual immorality just as often as men. You add this to women being victims of sex trafficking and also being taken advantage of in the pornography industries, and you have a much worse situation for women than for men. Either way, the hearts and minds of humanity are being destroyed by sexual addiction and misconduct. I feel we often focus on the men when we talk about the sprit of Jezebel and forget how it has corrupted and harmed women as well.

Sad to say, this is not just a worldly issue. It is every bit as present in the lives of Christians as it is in the lives of non-Christians. Unfortunately, the modern day church seems to take no issue or even notice. Either the church is afraid to speak out against it, or the church doesn't care. Even worse, we are seeing churches all over America and all over the world embrace, and even celebrate, sexual immortality. I believe this is just another sign we are, in fact, living in the end of days.

In the Book of Revelation, we see Jesus rebuking the church of Thyatira for tolerating a woman named Jezebel who has seduced His servants to commit sexual immortality. As a result, Jesus pronounces judgement over Jezebel and over those who took part with her, and promises to cast them into "great tribulation." Do you see the seriousness of this? This sin is not taken lightly by the Messiah. This sin, this spirit of Jezebel, will not only destroy your life, but it will destroy your faith and your relationship with the Lord.

"Notwithstanding I have a few things against thee, because thou sufferest that woman Jezebel, which calleth herself a prophetess, to teach and to seduce my servants to commit fornication, and to eat things sacrificed unto idols. And I gave her space to repent of her fornication; and she repented not. Behold, I will cast her into a bed, and them that commit adultery with her into great tribulation, except they repent of their deeds. And I will kill her children with death; and all the churches shall know that I am he which searcheth the reins and hearts: and I will give unto every one of you according to your works."
Revelation 2:20-23 KJV

Listen to me, my brothers and sisters. We must flee from this wicked spirit! We must not partake with her! Lest we be thrown into a sick bed and into great tribulation. Lest everything important to us be destroyed. Our relationships, our faith, and our reputation. Most importantly, lest we become a fornicator, or profane person, as Esau, who for one morsel of meat sold his very birthright. (See Hebrews 12:16 KJV)

THIS IS A VERY SERIOUS ISSUE, and I would argue the most destructive problem in Christianity today. The spirit of Jezebel, the spirit of sexual immorality, is corrupting the minds of our youth, our men, our women and even our churches. We must resist, we must repent, and may God have mercy on us and forgive us of these great trespasses.

> "But unto you I say, and unto the rest in Thyatira, as many as have not this doctrine, and which have not known the depths of Satan, as they speak; I will put upon you none other burden. But that which ye have already hold fast till I come." Revelation 2:24-25 KJV

26

THE SPIRIT OF JEZEBEL - PART 2

DAY 26

Unfortunately, sexual immorality is just not taken seriously by the modern day church. In many cases, it's embraced, and sometimes even celebrated. This should not be so. As the great Apostle Paul wrote, the sin of fornication or sexual immorality should not be named among God's people!

> "**But fornication**, and all uncleanness, or covetousness, let it not be once named among you, as becometh saints; Neither filthiness, nor foolish talking, nor jesting, which are not convenient: but rather giving of thanks." Ephesians 5:3-4 KJV

The question then becomes, "How do we overcome this immortality?" We live in a world where temptation is around every corner. If you go to the grocery store, you will see flesh, half-naked people, dressed incredibly inappropriate. You will see billboards and posters of men and women in their underwear. Even if you sit down to watch television, you will see commercials and movie trailers showing great sexual immorality in graphic detail. The same goes for movies, social media, and video games. Everywhere we look is the temptation to lust, and this sin is not one to take lightly. Jesus taught lusting after a woman does not differ from committing the actual act of adultery.

> "Ye have heard that it was said by them of old time, Thou shalt not commit adultery: But I say unto you, **That whosoever looketh on a woman to lust after her hath committed adultery** with her already in his heart."
> Matthew 5:27-28 KJV

The first thing we need to acknowledge and understand about the temptation of lust is it starts with our eye. Not in the heart and mind, but in the eye. Notice Jesus said, "whosoever looketh." Right after the above statement, Jesus says something even more radical about the importance of overcoming sexual immorality.

> "And if thy right eye offend thee, pluck it out, and cast it from thee: for it is profitable for thee that one of thy members should perish, and not that thy whole body should be cast into hell." Matthew 5:29 KJV

What does our Messiah mean when he says, *"and if thy right eye offend thee, pluck it out?"* Is Jesus literally telling us to gouge our eye out in order to avoid lust? I would argue Jesus is trying to tell us we must cut the sin off at the root. We must cut out the things which can lead us into sexual sin.

Jesus makes it very clear how important it is to do so. *"For it is profitable for thee that one of thy members should perish, and not that thy whole body should be cast into hell."*

This is a very serious statement many Christians overlook. According to Jesus, failing to overcome can lead us right into hell.

The sin starts with the eye and we must cut it off at the source, at the root. This could mean we may not be able to trust ourselves with things like social media. Reason being, there are several forms of social media which are mostly filled with sexually inappropriate images. There are even a couple of social media platforms which make pornography openly and willingly available.

This means even if you're not looking for trouble, the enemy can bring it before your eyes. We must cut it off! It might mean we no longer have cable or streaming services which provide tempting content that contains sexual immorality. Admittedly, it may not be fun or comfortable to do these things. It may not always be easy to LOOK AWAY when you are out and about and you see Jezebel walking your direction. However, the consequences of these sins are grave and much is at stake.

YOU MUST NEVER GIVE UP. If you fail, repent and start again. You must finish the race and finish it well. There is no pleasure of the eye worth sacrificing your inheritance for. There is no sin of the eye worth ruining your reputation and destroying your marriage for. Resolve in your heart, to not even look, and to cut the sin off at the source. May God have mercy on us in this and give us the strength to be overcomers through the power of the Holy Spirit. Amen.

"Know ye not that the unrighteous shall not inherit the kingdom of God? **Be not deceived: neither fornicators,** nor idolaters, nor adulterers, nor effeminate, nor abusers of themselves with mankind, Nor thieves, nor covetous, nor drunkards, nor revilers, nor extortioners, shall inherit the kingdom of God. And such were some of you: but ye are washed, but ye are sanctified, but ye are justified in the name of the Lord Jesus, and by the Spirit of our God." 1 Corinthians 6:9-11 KJV

GOD GAVE THEM OVER TO A REPROBATE MIND

DAY 27

I n these last days, we are seeing a massive increase in wickedness and ungodliness which shouldn't come as much of a surprise to us. As a culture moves further and further away from God, they raise up for themselves new gods, false gods. Or they themselves become a god in their own eyes. I believe the latter is more true today.

On the Western world stage, God has been exiled from all parts of the public eye. We have removed Him from our public schools, our universities, and our government. We now celebrate every form of wickedness and perversion in these institutions. Meanwhile, these same institutions openly despise Jesus Christ, along with His followers.

The scriptures tell us that when a society chooses to no longer retain God in their knowledge, when they move on to false gods, He will then give them up to their wicked passions and sins. He will give them over to a reprobate mind which will lead to them fulfilling all the evil in their hearts and to do things which are unnatural and ungodly.

When a society is given over to this reprobate mind, they become sexually immoral, they begin to hate God, they become proud. They lack mercy and become increasingly deceitful. Even their children will be disobedient and disrespectful.

Does this sound familiar to you? Sadly, I believe it sounds exactly like the culture we are living in today.

> "And even as they did not like to retain God in their knowledge, God gave them over to a reprobate mind, to do those things which are not convenient; Being filled with all unrighteousness, fornication, wickedness, covetousness, maliciousness; full of envy, murder, debate, deceit, malignity; whisperers, Backbiters, haters of God, despiteful, proud, boasters, inventors of evil things, disobedient to parents, Without understanding, covenantbreakers, without natural affection, implacable, unmerciful." Romans 1:28-31 KJV

The scriptures go on to tell us, God's judgement is coming upon these people. Those who walk in this ungodliness and have refused to retain Him in their knowledge. Not only them, but those who also take pleasure in their ungodliness. There may be those who don't commit wicked sexual sin with their own body, but take pleasure in watching it on television or hearing about it from a friend. There may be those who don't lie and cheat others, but find it amusing when it happens to someone they dislike. Judgement is also coming for them. Celebrating sin is just as wicked as committing it yourself. God is looking at the heart, is He not?

> "Who knowing the judgment of God, that they which commit such things are worthy of death, **not only do the**

same, but have pleasure in them that do them." Romans 1:32 KJV

We must set ourselves apart from this ungodly world. We must be sure to keep the knowledge of God in our hearts and minds and to teach it to our children. We must shout the good news of Jesus Christ from the rooftops! We must walk in righteousness and holiness, setting an example to this wicked generation. We must be the light on the hilltop, the salt to the earth as our Master has so lovingly instructed us to do.

LORD, help us walk the path of uprightness. May we never take pleasure in those who commit such evil things worthy of death. Instead, may we show them the love of our Messiah and the freedom from sin which only comes by a relationship with You. Amen.

28

WE MUST ENDURE TO THE END

DAY 28

I t's one thing to start a race, but it's an entirely different thing to finish. We see clearly in the scriptures starting is not enough. We must finish, we must endure, we must persevere to the end if we wish to be saved.

"Then shall they deliver you up to be afflicted, and shall kill you: and ye shall be hated of all nations for my name's sake. And then shall many be offended, and shall betray one another, and shall hate one another. And many false prophets shall rise, and shall deceive many. And because iniquity shall abound, the love of many shall wax cold. **But he that shall endure unto the end, the same shall be saved.** And this gospel of the kingdom shall be preached in all the world for a witness unto all nations; and then shall the end come." Matthew 24:9-14 KJV

This may seem obvious to many of us. However, as we move deeper and deeper into these last days, life will get harder and harder for the believer. Finishing the race of faith may prove to be more difficult than most might have expected. In the scriptures we see Jesus reminding the church of Smyrna to endure, to persevere to the end, and to be faithful even unto death. This reminder was followed with a promise of eternal life and reward if they do finish strong.

> "Fear none of those things which thou shalt suffer: behold, the devil shall cast some of you into prison, that ye may be tried; and ye shall have tribulation ten days: **be thou faithful unto death, and I will give thee a crown of life.**"
> Revelation 2:10 KJV

I can't help but wonder and ask myself, should we be so arrogant and ignorant as to think our Messiah would allow such suffering in the lives of His early followers and disciples, but allow us to only live in comfort? To live a life free of persecution and suffering for His namesake? I fear we have become too comfortable and I tremble at how inept the modern Christian might be at dealing with suffering, especially for the sake of the faith. How many of us are truly willing to stand firm in our faith in the face of death or great injury to ourselves or our families?

However, it's not only trials and tribulation which cause us to lose faith. The more likely reason one may stumble and not finish this race is because they are drawn away by sin and by their own evil hearts. We must guard against this every day! The lures of sin and the deceptions of the great adversary are very subtle. We must flee from those temptations as if our very lives and eternal futures depend on it because they do! Despite what the modern church might tell us, our actions do, in fact, matter.

> "Take heed, brethren, lest there be in any of you an evil

heart of unbelief, in departing from the living God. But exhort one another daily, while it is called To day; lest any of you be hardened through the deceitfulness of sin. **For we are made partakers of Christ, if we hold the beginning of our confidence stedfast unto the end;** While it is said, To day if ye will hear his voice, harden not your hearts, as in the provocation." Hebrews 3:12-15 KJV

MAY we be like the great Apostle Paul, reaching the end of our lives, knowing with confidence, we have kept the faith and finished the race. May we long for our Messiah, His appearing, and the Crown of Righteousness awaiting us. Praise the living God and His Son, Jesus Christ, our merciful Savior.

"For I am now ready to be offered, and the time of my departure is at hand. **I have fought a good fight, I have finished my course, I have kept the faith:** Henceforth there is laid up for me a crown of righteousness, which the Lord, the righteous judge, shall give me at that day: and not to me only, but unto all them also that love his appearing." 2 Timothy 4:6-8 KJV

29

DON'T FORSAKE GATHERING
TOGETHER IN THESE LAST DAYS

The perseverance of the faith and our walk with Messiah was never meant to be endured alone. Instead, we are called to walk side-by-side with our fellow brothers and sisters in the faith. We are commanded to care for one another's needs, to love one another, and bless and support one another.

In fact, the scriptures tell us the world will recognize we belong to the Messiah because of the love we share for one another.

> "By this shall all men know that ye are my disciples, if ye have love one to another." John 13:35 KJV

However, I'm not so sure this is what we see amongst believers today. For most, the only interaction we have with our brothers and sisters in Christ is a nod, a smile or maybe a handshake at church on Sunday.

This should not be so! We should gather in our homes, tend to one another, and encourage one another in the faith. We should break bread and share each other's burdens.

Unfortunately, the church today and the attitude of the believer are far different from what we see in the book of Acts.

> "And the multitude of them that believed were of one heart and of one soul: neither said any of them that ought of the things which he possessed was his own; but they had all things common. And with great power gave the apostles witness of the resurrection of the Lord Jesus: and great grace was upon them all. **Neither was there any among them that lacked: for as many as were possessors of lands or houses sold them, and brought the prices of the things that were sold, And laid them down at the apostles' feet: and distribution was made unto every man according as he had need."** Acts 4:32-35 KJV

Can you image a church body today willing to sell their own possessions, lands, and more to provide for the needs of their less fortunate brothers and sisters in Christ? This concept probably seems ridiculous and unfathomable to most of us.

Now, please understand, I'm not saying you have to go sell your house and give the proceeds to a corporate church. What I'm trying to get across is the attitude of the early believers toward one another. They had an attitude of great love for their brethren. The early believers gathered often. They cared for one another often, not just for an hour on Sunday morning. Many believers don't even attend church anymore, much less gather in homes throughout the week.

Now, you need not attend some modern day, apostate, corporate-style church. However, we should gather with like-minded followers of our Messiah. We must resist the temptation to isolate ourselves from our fellow brothers and sisters in the faith. Especially as we are moving into the last days. In fact, the scriptures warn us against this practice. Why? Because as things heat up and the hostility continues to grow toward true followers of Jesus, we will need each other more than ever if we hope to endure to the end.

"Let us draw near with a true heart in full assurance of faith, having our hearts sprinkled from an evil conscience, and our bodies washed with pure water. Let us hold fast the profession of our faith without wavering; (for he is faithful that promised;) And let us consider one another to provoke unto love and to good works: **Not forsaking the assembling of ourselves together, as the manner of some is; but exhorting one another: and so much the more, as ye see the day approaching.** For if we sin wilfully after that we have received the knowledge of the truth, there remaineth no more sacrifice for sins, But a certain fearful looking for of judgment and fiery indignation, which shall devour the adversaries." Hebrews 10:22-27 KJV

As we see the day approaching, the return of our Messiah on the horizon, may we be more intentional about gathering together. May we be more sacrificial with our love, our possessions, and our time. Let us be as the true remnant church, the church Jesus commanded us to be.

30

WHERE IS HIS COMING?

DAY 30

A s we look at the world, the injustice, the perversions, the wickedness, and ungodliness, it can be very tempting to get discouraged. After all, where is His coming? Why hasn't He put an end to all the suffering? Where is all His promises and the fulfillment thereof?

The scriptures reassure us God is not slow or slack on delivering on His promises, at least not in the way we would measure slackness. The reason for His delay is His great mercy and great love for humanity. He delays simply because He wants all to come to the knowledge of the truth and to be saved.

"The Lord is not slack concerning his promise, as some men count slackness; but is longsuffering to us-ward, not willing that any should perish, but that all should come to repentance." 2 Peter 3:9 KJV

However, there is coming a point in time, which I believe is very near, where His patience and long-suffering will come to an end and judgement will arrive. It will surely come, and it will come swiftly and quickly. Most people will be taken off guard. Many who call themselves Christians will not be prepared.

His appearing will come like a thief in the night, and this old wicked world will be burned up by fire. Knowing all this, the scriptures tell us to consider what type of people we ought to be. We need to ask ourselves, am I walking in righteousness and holiness? Am I walking according to His commandments? Am I ready to meet Him today?

> "But the day of the Lord will come as a thief in the night; in the which the heavens shall pass away with a great noise, and the elements shall melt with fervent heat, the earth also and the works that are therein shall be burned up. **Seeing then that all these things shall be dissolved, what manner of persons ought ye to be in all holy conversation and godliness, Looking for and hasting unto the coming of the day of God, wherein the heavens being on fire shall be dissolved, and the elements shall melt with fervent heat?** Nevertheless we, according to his promise, look for new heavens and a new earth, wherein dwelleth righteousness." 2 Peter 3:10-13 KJV

We need to keep our heads up, stay positive and look up with great expectation of His coming. Let us not put our hopes and dreams in this decaying world of wickedness. Rather, let us hope in the new heavens and the new earth where only righteousness exist, where He will dwell with us for all eternity.

> "And, behold, I come quickly; and my reward is with me, to give every man according as his work shall be. I am

Alpha and Omega, the beginning and the end, the first and the last. Blessed are they that do his commandments, that they may have right to the tree of life, and may enter in through the gates into the city. For without are dogs, and sorcerers, and whoremongers, and murderers, and idolaters, and whosoever loveth and maketh a lie." Revelation 22:12-15 KJV

MAY His mercy and grace be upon us. May He strengthen us to finish this race of faith and endure until the end. May we never lose hope in His promises and may we all delight in His final return. Praise the living God, praise the Lord Jesus.

"He which testifieth these things saith, Surely I come quickly. Amen. Even so, come, Lord Jesus." Revelation 22:20 KJV

CLOSING THOUGHTS

I almost didn't write this book. Here we are in the year 2020 and I've felt lead to write a book for at least 6 years. I always thought to myself, "What's the point? The world is burning down around us, and time is short."

I believed because of the events unfolding in the world, our Messiah would surely return at any minute. I thought if our Savior didn't return soon, the world would be in such chaos that taking the time to write and publish a book about the end of days would be a foolish waste of time. I couldn't have been more wrong.

Something I've learned over the years is God isn't in a hurry. His plans will come to pass at exactly the right time. In the meantime, our job is to be salt and a light to this fallen world. We are to minister to the poor and needy. We are to share the good news of Jesus with those who are lost and in need of hope.

I see three types of Christians today.

The first type of Christian is completely oblivious to what's going on in the world. They are carnal-minded and live and act just like the rest of modern society. Yes, they believe, but they can't fathom anything bad might happen, and the fact that the End Times might be upon us. They are not interested in the conversation; they don't want this world to pass because they love this world.

The second type of Christian I see today are those who are awake to the notion something is wrong. They can see the world is moving in a very negative direction. However, they respond with fear. Afraid to go out of their homes, always watching the news and stressing out about each and every piece of propaganda coming through the television.

The third type is what I call the remnant Christian. These are few in numbers. These make it a priority to walk in righteousness and holiness. These Christians spend their mornings on their knees praying and seeking God's face. These Christians are not interested in looking and acting like the world, much less partaking in the world's ways of ungodliness. They know the times are upon us. They know the end must be near, but instead of being paralyzed by fear, they are moved to work and take action. They are DOING things for the Kingdom of God. They share the good news and tend to those in need. They have committed their life to Jesus and the mission of the gospel.

I ask you now, which Christian are you in these very last days? Are you a denier? Are you a coward? Or are you part of the remnant of God, a soldier of Messiah in these last days?

We are called to be a salt to this earth. The interesting thing about salt is, once it's sprinkled on something, it cannot be undone. Salt leaves a permanent and lasting taste on whatever is being seasoned. Try as you might, you cannot undo it. This is the impact we are to have on this world. This might mean we have to get uncomfortable. We might have to take some chances and put ourselves at risk for the sake of the gospel.

This is why Jesus tells us to take up our cross daily. It's difficult; it's supposed to be. Following the Messiah will cost you something. Is it not worth it? The days might come upon us when we have to make a definitive choice. Will you follow Jesus, or the world?

Let us not be cowards, but be the salt. Let us not hide away in our homes. Instead, may we be the hands and feet of our Messiah. Yes, the end of days are near and maybe at the door. All the more reason this is not the time to hide in a bunker somewhere with canned food. This is the time to partake in the bringing in of the largest harvest of souls in human history. Take action!

Could it be, maybe we were born for a time such as this?

"For if thou altogether holdest thy peace at this time, then shall there enlargement and deliverance arise to the Jews from another place; but thou and thy father's house shall be destroyed: **and who knoweth whether thou art come to the kingdom for such a time as this?**" Esther 4:14 KJV

ABOUT SHAWN OZBUN

Shawn L. Ozbun is an independent podcaster, author, and commentator of many biblical topics, most notably eschatology. Shawn is a student of the scriptures, ancient writings and biblical Hebrew language. He focuses primarily on End Times prophecy, biblical history, apocryphal text, and the Dead Sea Scrolls. Most importantly, Shawn is passionate about delivering the gospel of Jesus Christ.

Shawn loves to both read and write devotionals based on the scriptures he loves so dearly. You can receive his weekly email devotional by signing up at http://scriptureandprophecy.com

RESOURCES

Scripture and Prophecy Podcast
http://scriptureandprophecy.com/podcast-player/

Free Biblical Hebrew For Beginners Training Course
http://scriptureandprophecy.com/Hebrew

The KJV Bible I personally use - http://scriptureandprophecy.com/kjv

The Apocrypha I personally use - http://scriptureandprophecy.com/apocrypha

FOLLOW ON SOCIAL MEDIA

Facebook - http://facebook.com/truthfed

YouTube - http://scriptureandprophecy.com/youtube

Bitchute - http://scriptureandprophecy.com/bitchute

iTunes - http://scriptureandprophecy.com/itunes

ACKNOWLEDGMENTS

Patreon Subscribers

Thank you so much! This book would not be possible without your support. Your generosity also makes the YouTube content and podcast available as well. You are the reason I can do this great work. I'm so blessed and thankful for you! https://www.patreon.com/truthfed

PayPal & Mail Supporters

Thank you so much! Just like the Patreon supporters, your support makes all this possible. Some of you have supported me since the very beginning! I thank you for the kind letters I have received over the years as well as your amazing generosity. http://scriptureandprophecy.com/support/

My Wife, Melia

I also want to thank my beautiful wife Melia for all her

support and help with this project. Thank you for helping me with the edits and proofreading. Lord knows, I needed that help desperately. Thank you for believing in me.

COMING SOON

Coming Soon!
   The Book of Revelation 30 Day Devotional
   Estimated publication date December 2020

Sign up for email updates by joining the email list at
http://scriptureandprophecy.com

Printed in Great Britain
by Amazon

18578788R00068